Susan Goodman • Sandy Hammer

ACTION BOOKS

TECHNOLOGY

Published by
New Look Books
PO Box 864
Oxford
OX2 9YD

© New Look Books Ltd 1996, Reprinted 1997.

All rights reserved. No part of this publication may be reproduced, stored in a retrieval system, or transmitted, in any form or by any means, electronic, mechanical, photocopying, recording or otherwise, without the written permission of the publishers.

ISBN 1-901308-01-4

British Library Cataloguing in Publication Data.
A catalogue record for this book is available from the British Library.

Printed and bound in Great Britain.

Rocket riddle

Find one letter from each of the clues in this riddle.
They spell out a word connected with space travel.

my first is in **Mars** but not in **space**
my second is in **probe** but not in **race**
my third is in **craft** but not in **star**
my fourth is in **Lunik** but not in **lunar**
my fifth is in **planet** and in **pole**
my sixth is in **hot** but not in **hole**
put me together and up you go

If BZLMXTXERM stands for ASTRONOMER
what is the code for:

STAR   MOON   ROTATE

DO YOU KNOW?
It is extremely expensive to build a rocket and use it only once. The Americans invented a much cheaper system. They built a space plane or shuttle, which flies into space and returns to earth many times. The only part that is wasted is the large fuel tank. Even the two booster rockets which help lift the shuttle into space have parachutes so that they fall gently down into the sea and are collected by ships. The first shuttle flight was on 12 April 1981.

Flying high

Here are some record heights.

Find the difference in height between Mount Everest and the hot-air balloon altitude record.

How much higher is the balloon record than Concorde?

19,811m — In 1988 Per Linstrad reached a record height in a hot-air balloon.

15,240m — Concorde on a transatlantic flight. The triangular wing shape, called a delta, is good for high-speed flight. Concorde, designed in the 1960s, was the first supersonic passenger plane.

8,848m — Mount Everest. The highest mountain in the world.

DO YOU KNOW?

The higher you go the colder it gets. At about 10,000m above sea level it is always as cold as winter at the South Pole, about -55°C.

To the point

Solve these decimal problems and write the answer in each hot-air balloon.

- 34.3 − 5.8
- 29.4 + 3.9
- 23.2 − 0.9
- 7.4 − 3.1
- 26 ÷ 10
- 21.2 + 1.3
- 4.4 + 6.7
- 6.8 + 2.3
- 7.6 − 2.1
- 9.2 + 2.9
- 16.7 − 8.4
- 32.8 + 16.6
- 9.4 − 5.9
- 43 ÷ 10

DO YOU KNOW?

The first balloon to carry living things was built in France by the two Montgolfier brothers. A duck, a sheep and a rooster flew in 1788 in the basket of a balloon for eight minutes and then landed safely.

Bicycling

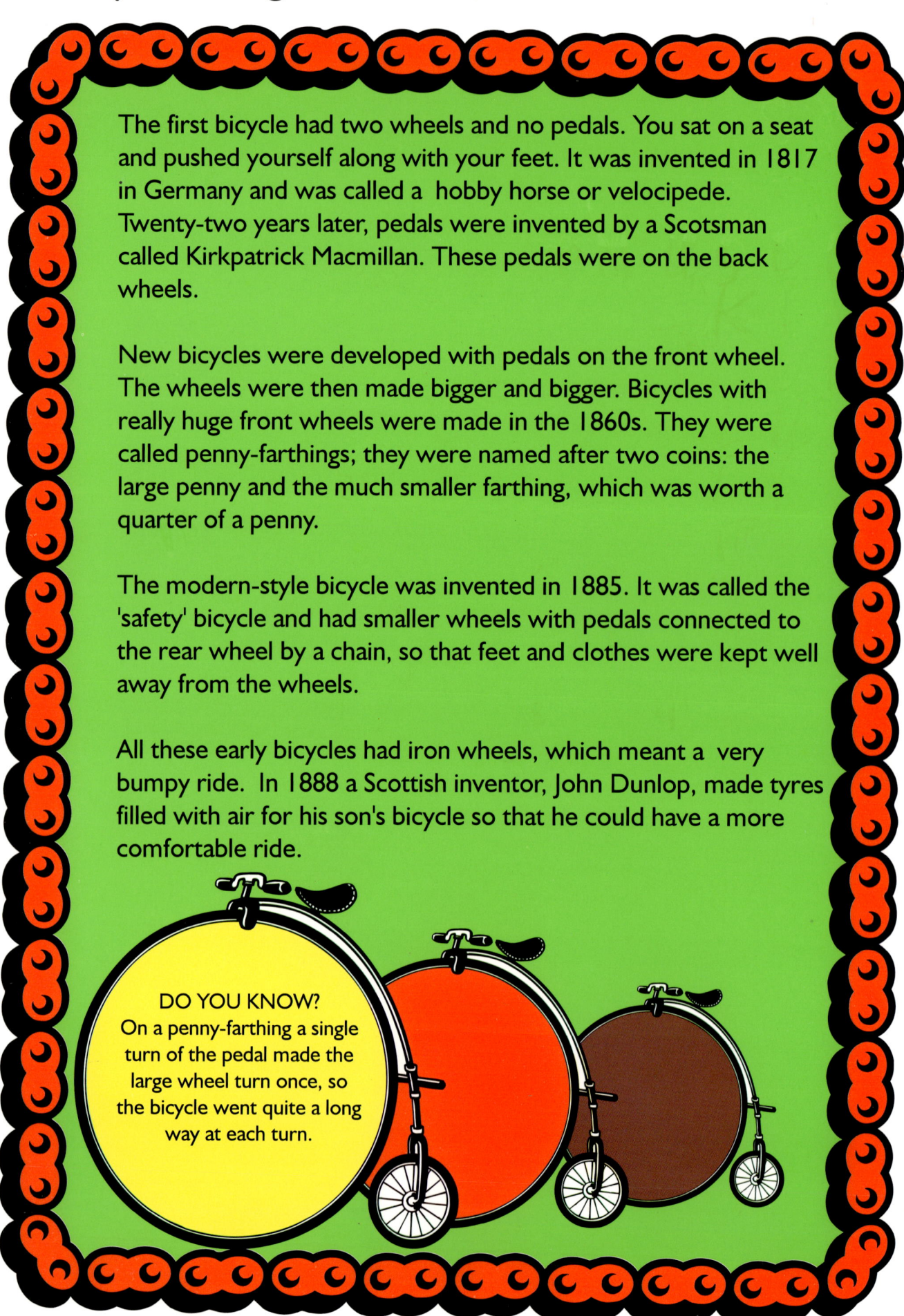

The first bicycle had two wheels and no pedals. You sat on a seat and pushed yourself along with your feet. It was invented in 1817 in Germany and was called a hobby horse or velocipede. Twenty-two years later, pedals were invented by a Scotsman called Kirkpatrick Macmillan. These pedals were on the back wheels.

New bicycles were developed with pedals on the front wheel. The wheels were then made bigger and bigger. Bicycles with really huge front wheels were made in the 1860s. They were called penny-farthings; they were named after two coins: the large penny and the much smaller farthing, which was worth a quarter of a penny.

The modern-style bicycle was invented in 1885. It was called the 'safety' bicycle and had smaller wheels with pedals connected to the rear wheel by a chain, so that feet and clothes were kept well away from the wheels.

All these early bicycles had iron wheels, which meant a very bumpy ride. In 1888 a Scottish inventor, John Dunlop, made tyres filled with air for his son's bicycle so that he could have a more comfortable ride.

DO YOU KNOW?
On a penny-farthing a single turn of the pedal made the large wheel turn once, so the bicycle went quite a long way at each turn.

True or false

	TRUE	FALSE
Bicycles have always had two wheels.	✓	☐
The first bicycle was invented over 200 years ago.	☐	✓
A Scotsman called John Dunlop invented pedals.	☐	✓
The first pedals were on the back wheel.	✓	☐
The penny-farthing bicycle was given its name because it was cheap to buy.	✓	☐
Inflated tyres were invented 71 years after the invention of the bicycle.	✓	☐
The 'safety' bicycle was so called because it had chains round the wheels to grip the road.	☐	✓

DO YOU KNOW?
The word bicycle comes from two words. The word *bis*, which is Latin, meaning 'twice', and the Greek work *kuklos* meaning 'wheel'.

Body parts

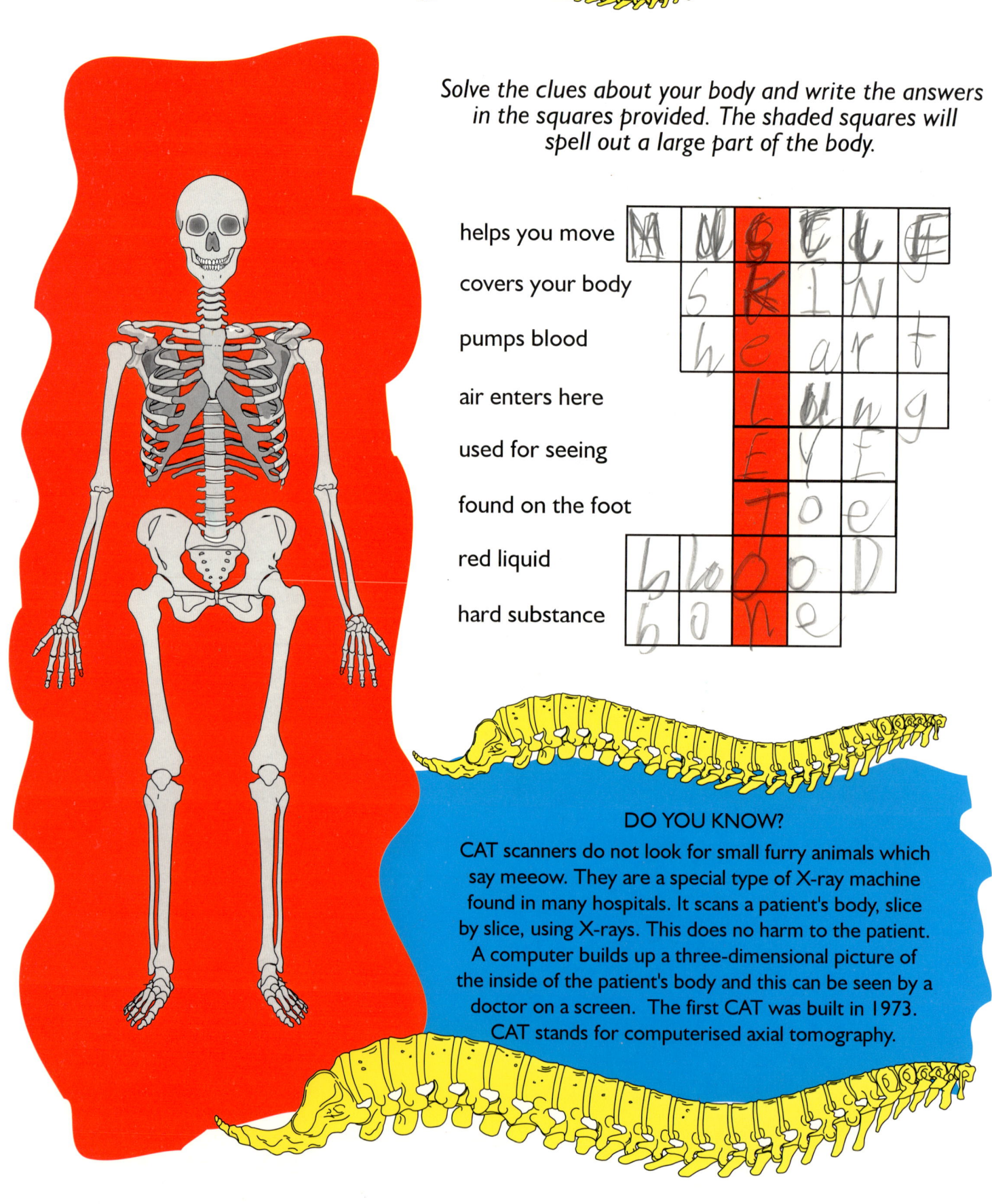

Solve the clues about your body and write the answers in the squares provided. The shaded squares will spell out a large part of the body.

clue	answer
helps you move	MUSCLE
covers your body	SKIN
pumps blood	heart
air enters here	lung
used for seeing	EYE
found on the foot	toe
red liquid	blood
hard substance	bone

(Shaded squares spell: SKELETON)

DO YOU KNOW?

CAT scanners do not look for small furry animals which say meeow. They are a special type of X-ray machine found in many hospitals. It scans a patient's body, slice by slice, using X-rays. This does no harm to the patient. A computer builds up a three-dimensional picture of the inside of the patient's body and this can be seen by a doctor on a screen. The first CAT was built in 1973. CAT stands for computerised axial tomography.

Keep cool

A nurse takes the temperature of a patient every three hours. The temperature is measured in degrees Celsius (°C). Normal temperature is about 37°C. Here is the patient's temperature chart for 24 hours.

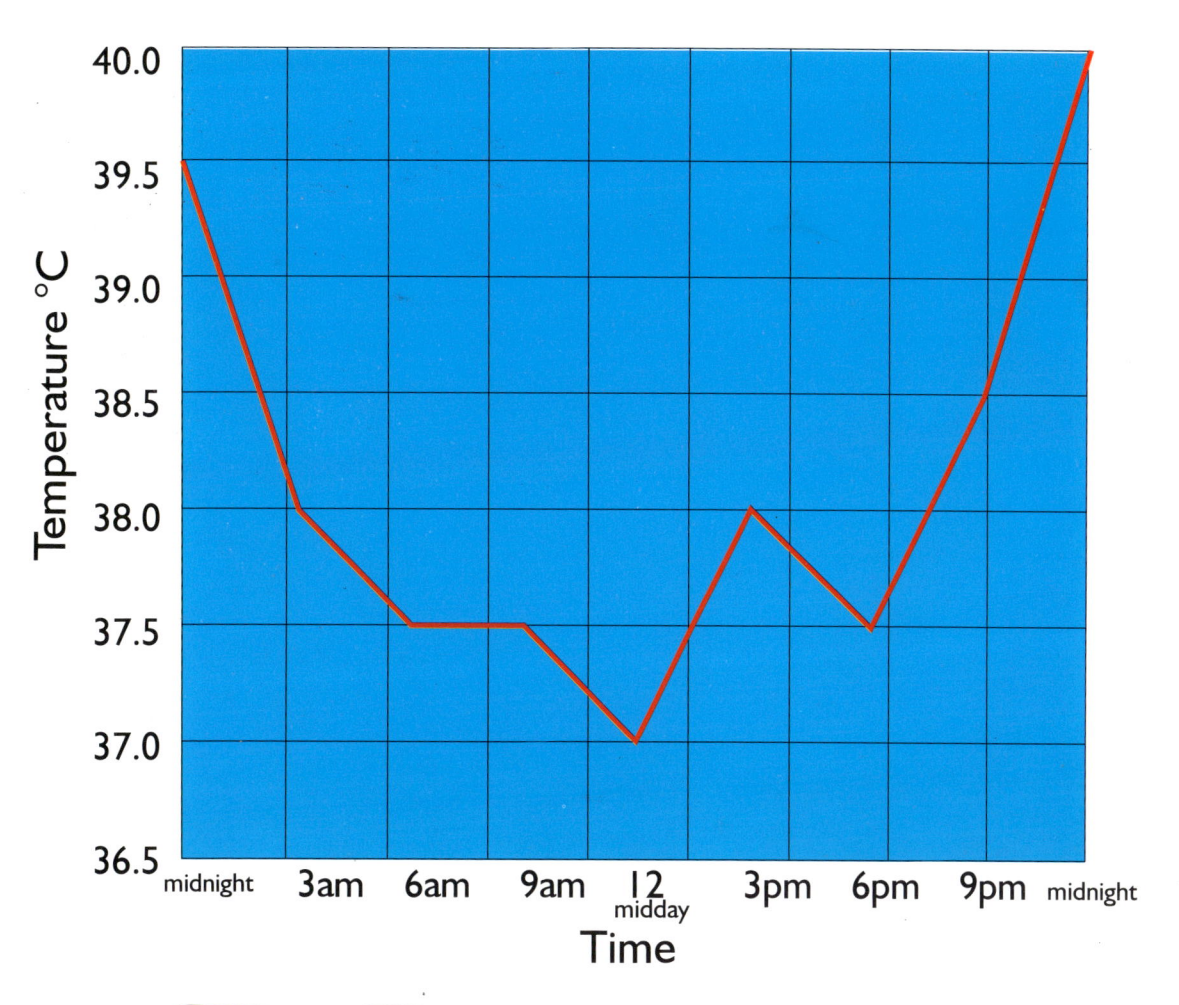

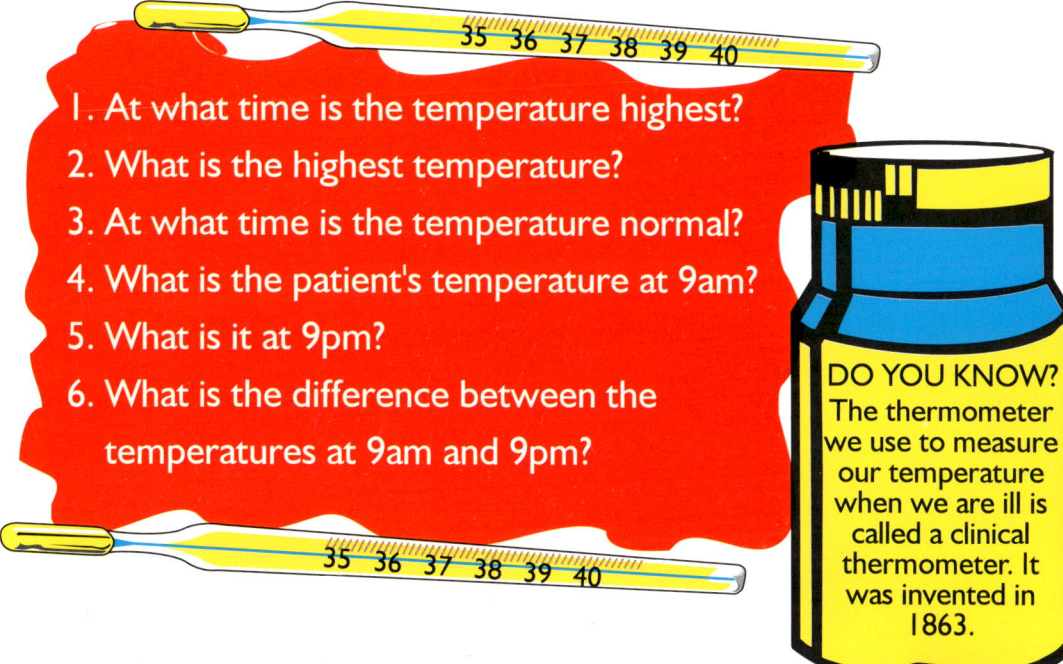

1. At what time is the temperature highest?
2. What is the highest temperature?
3. At what time is the temperature normal?
4. What is the patient's temperature at 9am?
5. What is it at 9pm?
6. What is the difference between the temperatures at 9am and 9pm?

DO YOU KNOW? The thermometer we use to measure our temperature when we are ill is called a clinical thermometer. It was invented in 1863.

Computer confusion

All these jumbled words have something to do with computers. The rhyming word will give a clue what the word sounds like but not necessarily how it is spelt.

redahwra
ryhmes with bear

hpic
rhymes with flip

ybet
rhymes with night

seomu
rhymes with house

nerecs
rhymes with bean

remcoput
rhymes with hooter

marporg
rhymes with jam

rtnierp
rhymes with splinter

feswotar
rhymes with hair

Two by two

Computers store and process all sorts of information: numbers, words, pictures and colours. All of this is done by using a special code which has only two digits: 0 and 1. This is called the 'binary code'. 0 and 1 are called 'binary digits' or 'bits' for short.

Inside the computer there are tiny pulses of electricity which go through tiny electronic circuits on a chip. If a circuit has an electrical pulse it is a 1, if there is no pulse it is a 0.

Letters can be written in binary code with each letter represented as a series of eight bits. (Eight bits are called a 'byte'.)

Here are some letters written in binary code.
Work out the coded word below.

A	B	E	G	M	T	Y
0100001	01000010	01100010	10100010	11100010	10100011	11101010

11100010   01100010   10100010   0100001

01000010   11101010   10100011   01100010

DO YOU KNOW?

Chips are tiny slices of a substance called silicon. Some chips are so small they can pass through the eye of a needle. Each chip has millions of electric circuits on it.

Fast cars

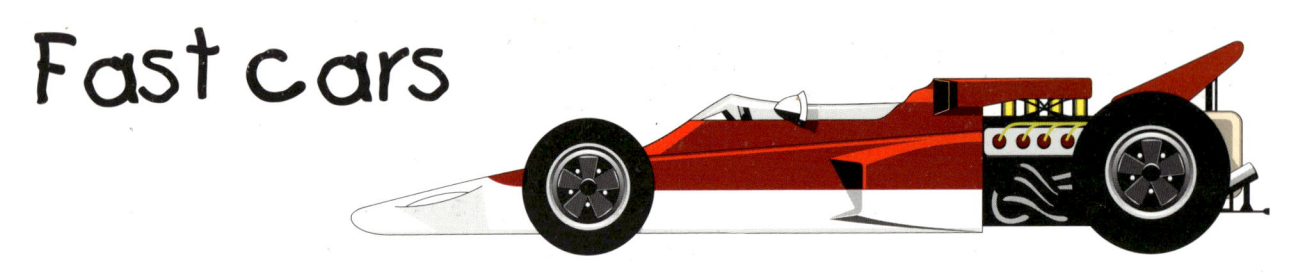

Today, in motor racing, average speeds of over 200mph are recorded. Single-lap records can reach over 230mph. The cars in the table below have held the land-speed records and are very different from racing cars. They are powered by rocket engines, with the exception of Thrust 2 which has a jet engine.

Date	Car	Driver	mph
1924	Bluebird	Sir Malcolm Campbell (GB)	146
1935	Bluebird	Sir Malcolm Campbell (GB)	300
1964	Bluebird	Donald Campbell (GB)	430
1970	Blue Flame	Gary Gabelich (USA)	622
1983	Thrust 2	Richard Noble (GB)	633

Quick change

5 miles = 8 kilometres
Therefore 5 mph = 8 km/h

To change miles per hour (mph) to kilometres per hour (km/h) divide by 5 and multiply by 8. Use your calculator to change all the speeds on this page from mph to km/h. Don't forget to change the racing car speeds at the top of the page.

Slow sums

Today we speed along motorways at speeds of up to 70 miles per hour. But the very first cars went at about the same speed as fast walking pace.

Look at the details below of some early cars and then work out some low-speed sums.

Inventor	Nationality	Type of Car	Date	Approximate top speed
1. Nicholas Cugnot	French	First steam car	1769	4 mph
2. Karl Benz	German	First petrol car	1885	8 mph
3. Henry Ford	USA	Petrol car	1896	24 mph

How long will it take for each of these cars to travel a distance of:

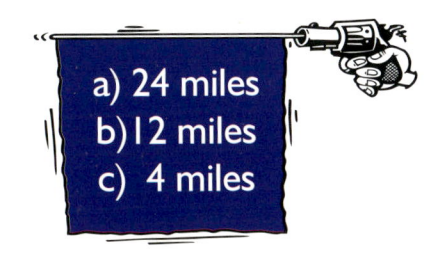

a) 24 miles
b) 12 miles
c) 4 miles

DO YOU KNOW?

In 1831, an Englishman, Sir Goldsworthy Gurney, invented a carriage powered by steam. It was used for a regular passenger service. Owners of horse-drawn transport felt threatened and persuaded the British Parliament to order that all power-driven vehicles must have a man walking in front holding a red flag. This meant motor cars had to travel slower than horse-drawn carriages.

TV TIMES

1.00 Good Cooks - with Henri and Jean Luc

1. At what time is the cookery programme? How long does it last?

2. It is 1pm. How long will you have to wait for the **News**?

3. How much time altogether is given to news programmes?

4. How long does **Children's TV** last?

5. Which is the longest programme on **Children's TV**.

6. If you watch from the **Six 0'Clock News** until the end of **Money Matters** how long will you have watched television.

12.30pm Lunchtime News
Weather

1.00 Good Cooks
Favourite recipes

1.40 Fun Fair
Fun and surprises for under-5s

2.40 A Stitch in Time
creative stitchwork

3.00   News

3.20 Children's TV
3.20 Mickey's World
3.50 Braintwister
4.15 Joke Box
4.30 Pet's Corner
5.00 Treasure Island

6.00 Six 0'Clock News
Weather

6.30 Science in Action
Latest reports from the world of science and technology

7.00 Suspect
Final episode of police thriller

7.30 Money Matters
An investment programme for all

8.00 Faraway
A holiday programme which will transport you to exotic locations

DO YOU KNOW?
In 1926 John Logie Baird gave the first public demonstration of television in London.

In the picture

Sort out the jumbled words shown in bold.

The first public showing of a film was in 1895 in Paris. The film was made by **wto** brothers, Auguste and Louis Lumière. They **detnevin** the cinematograph, a machine which was both a camera for taking the **srepitcu** and a projector for showing them on a **sneerc**. The cinematograph could only hold 16 metres of film. This meant that a film **dlesta** less than a **enitum**. These first films had titles such as *The Baby's Meal* and *The Arrival of a Train*. They were of course silent films.

The first sound film, called a 'talkie', was *The Jazz Singer,* shown in 1927. Within a few **rayes** all films had sound. Some of the **steb** actors in the silent films had to give up acting because **rheit** voices were not good enough.

DO YOU KNOW?

Film pictures appear to move on the screen. They are really still pictures flashing one after another. This happens very quickly and tricks your brain so that you seem to see movement.

Sail away

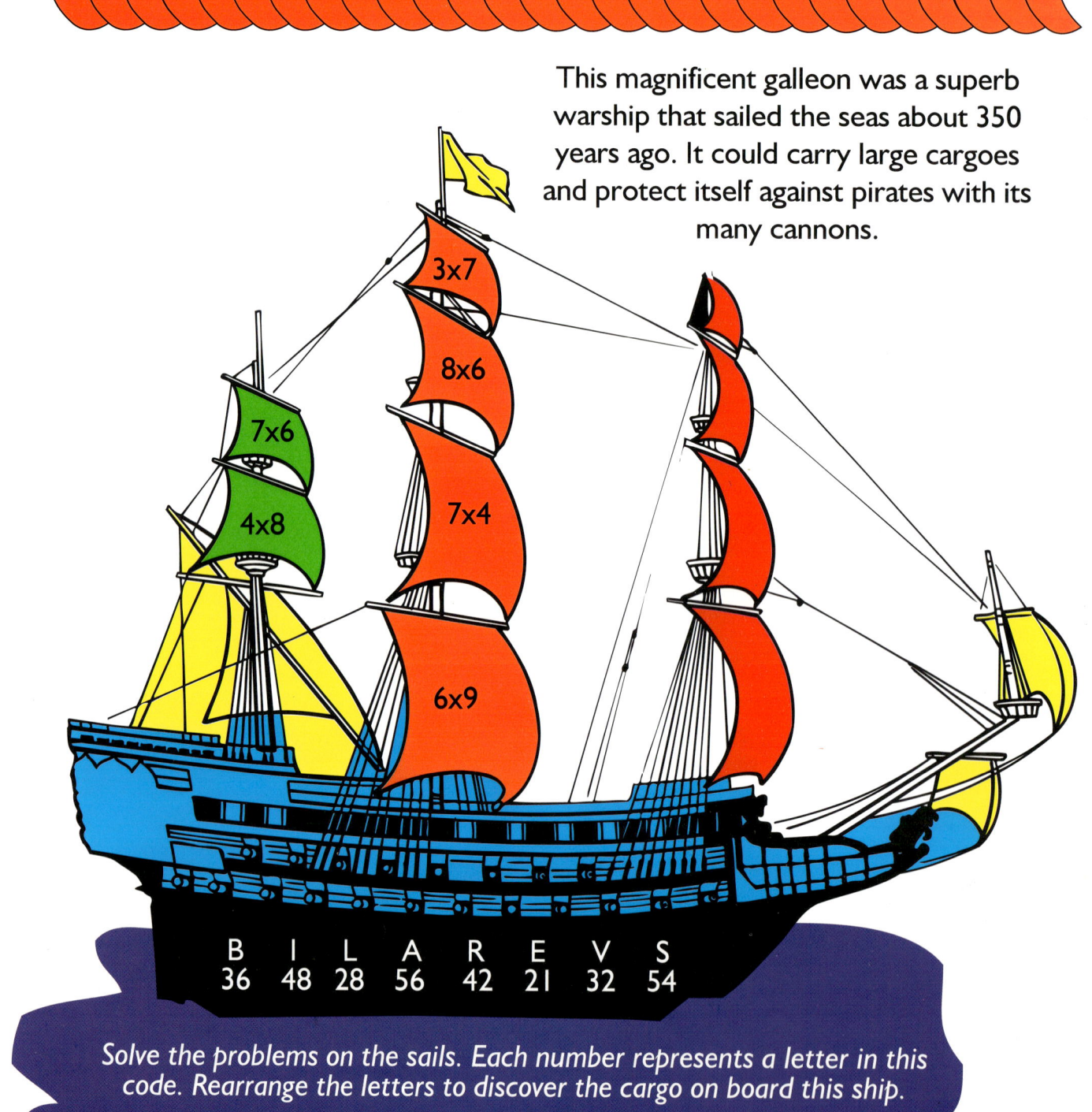

This magnificent galleon was a superb warship that sailed the seas about 350 years ago. It could carry large cargoes and protect itself against pirates with its many cannons.

Sails:
- 3x7
- 8x6
- 7x6
- 4x8
- 7x4
- 6x9

B	I	L	A	R	E	V	S
36	48	28	56	42	21	32	54

Solve the problems on the sails. Each number represents a letter in this code. Rearrange the letters to discover the cargo on board this ship.

DO YOU KNOW?
Galleons were the main ships of war for hundreds of years. They were eventually replaced by ships built of iron instead of wood and using steam power instead of sails.

Treasure hunt

Begin with the multiplication in the first lifebelt. Follow the rope with the correct answer to the next lifebelt. Keep going until you reach the treasure. Which treasure do you reach?

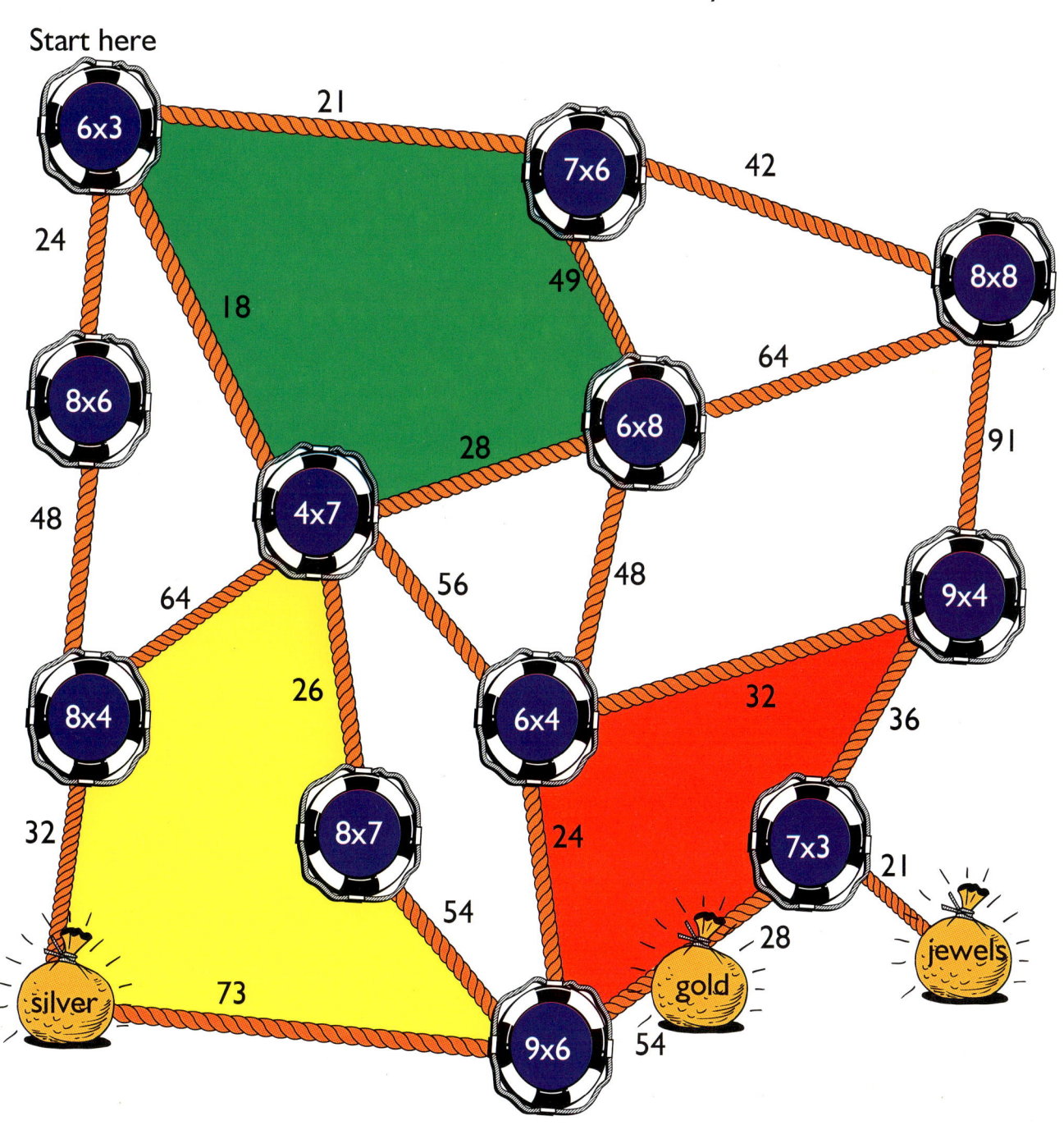

Start here

- 6×3 — 21, 24, 18
- 7×6 — 42, 49
- 8×8 — 64, 91
- 8×6 — 48
- 6×8 — 64, 28, 48
- 4×7 — 28, 56, 64
- 9×4 — 32, 36
- 8×4 — 32, 26
- 6×4 — 24, 54
- 8×7 — 54
- 7×3 — 21, 28
- 9×6 — 54, 73

silver — gold — jewels

Call costs

The tables that follow show the price per minute and examples of 5- and 10-minute calls. The price per minute varies depending on the time of day and the distance of the call. **Regional** is for a call up to 35 miles away, over 35 miles is **National. Local** is in the same town.

daytime (Mon to Fri 8am-6pm)

	local	regional	national
Price per min	4p	7p	9p
5 mins	20p	35p	45p
10mins	40p	70p	90p

evenings and night time (Mon to Fri before 8am and after 6pm)

	local	regional	national
Price per min	2p	4p	6p
5 mins	10p	20p	30p
10mins	20p	40p	60p

weekend (Midnight Fri- Midnight Sun)

	local	regional	national
Price per min	1p	3p	3p
5 mins	5p	15p	15p
10mins	10p	30p	30p

Work out the cost of the following phone calls.

1. Tom's teenage sister speaks to her boyfriend for one hour at 10pm Tuesday night. He lives round the corner.
2. Tom phones his cousin who lives a hundred miles away. He speaks for 5 minutes at 5.30pm on Saturday.
3. Tom's mother speaks to a friend for 30 minutes on Monday morning at 10am. She lives next door.
4. It is Friday. Tom's father calls his office at 9am and speaks for 25 minutes. His office is 20 miles away.

Telephone tangle

Each of the jumbled words has something to do with telephones. There is a clue to help you sort out what the word is.

mriheponco	you speak into this
belimo	a telephone you use on the move
itrensavocon	talking
enkwrot	system of many lines
erilcletac	worked by electricity
acotatimu	machine working on its own
utnotb	you press them to call someone
edomm	connects a computer to a telephone line

DO YOU KNOW?

The first telephones were built in 1876 by Alexander Graham Bell in the USA. He demonstrated it by speaking to his assistant, Watson, in the next room. Bell's first words on the telephone were: 'Mr Watson, come here! I want to see you.'

Electric wordsearch

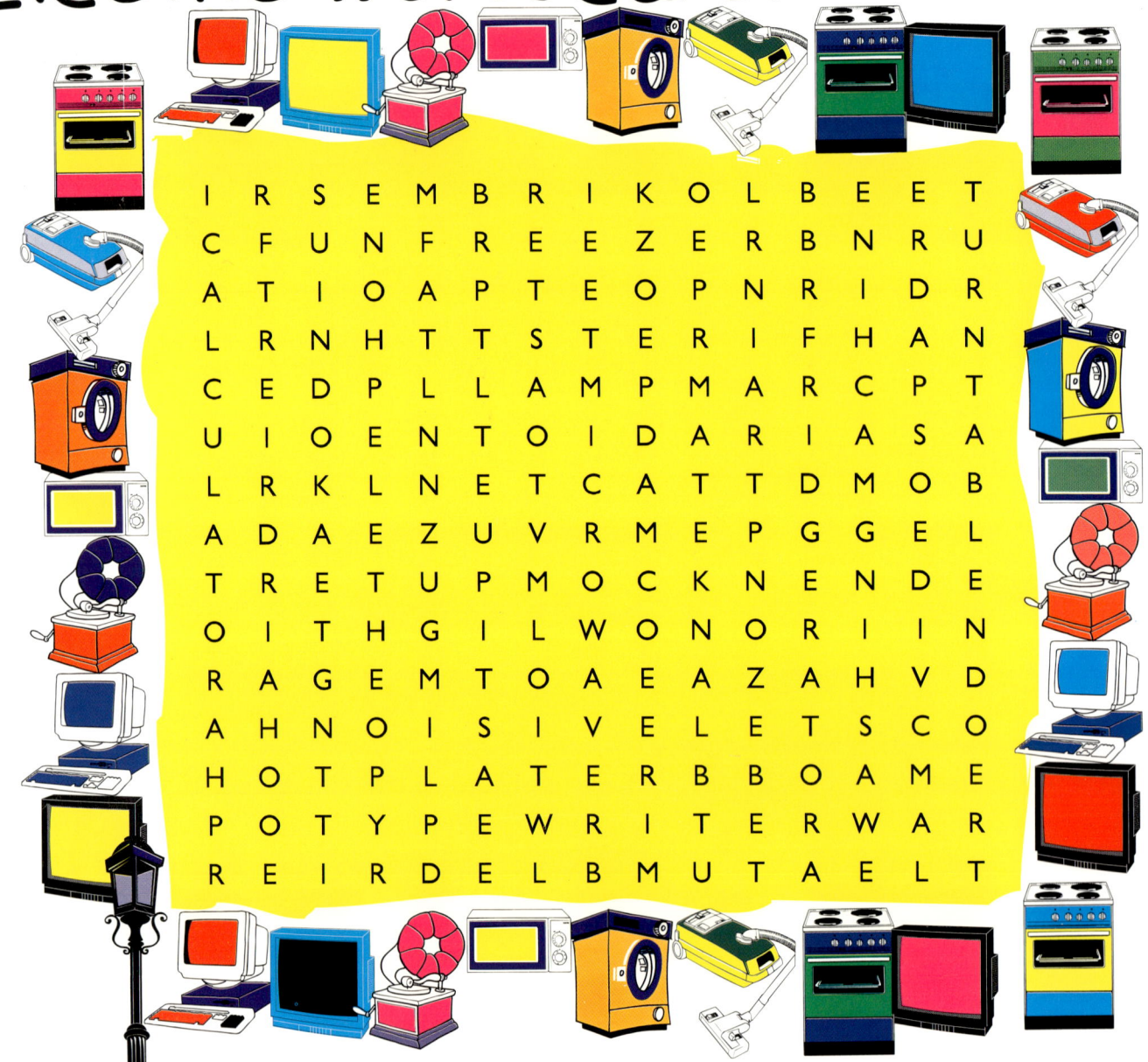

```
I R S E M B R I K O L B E E T
C F U N F R E E Z E R B N R U
A T I O A P T E O P N R I D R
L R N H T T S T E R I F H A N
C E D P L L A M P M A R C P T
U I O E N T O I D A R I A S A
L R K L N E T C A T T D M O B
A D A E Z U V R M E P G G E L
T R E T U P M O C K N E N D E
O I T H G I L W O N O R I I N
R A G E M T O A E A Z A H V D
A H N O I S I V E L E T S C O
H O T P L A T E R B B O A M E
P O T Y P E W R I T E R W A R
R E I R D E L B M U T A E L T
```

*Go forward, backwards, up, down and diagonally.
Find all these words.*

lamp	television	turntable
washing-machine	computer	typewriter
iron	fridge	train
toaster	freezer	calculator
kettle	blanket	motor
microwave	light	video
oven	fire	tumble-drier
telephone	hotplate	hairdrier
radio	car	hi-fi

Odd-one-out

Underline the odd-one-out in each group of words.

1. (refrigerator, toaster, freezer)
2. (oven, iron, washing-machine)
3. (record, microphone, cassette)
4. (microwave, iron, oven)
5. (television, radio, telephone)
6. (telephone, hi-fi, oven)
7. (light bulb, toaster, kettle)
8. (bicycle, car, motorcycle)

Underline the odd-one-out in each group of numbers.

a. (15, 3, 27, 4)
b. (6, 7, 16, 12)
c. (25, 13, 15, 40)
d. (81, 18, 8, 27)
e. (16, 7, 21, 49)
f. (88, 9, 16, 40)

DO YOU KNOW?

The first vacuum cleaner was made in 1901 by Hubert Booth. It was pulled by horse and left outside the house. A long tube was then passed into the house through the windows to suck up the dirt from carpets.

ANSWERS

Rocket riddle
rocket. ZLBM, EXXT, MXLBLR.

Flying high
10, 963m, 4,571m.

To the point
34.3-5.8=28.5, 29.4+3.9=33.3, 7.4-3.1=4.3, 6.8+2.3=9.1,
16.7-8.4=8.3, 43÷10=4.3, 9.4-5.9=3.5, 32.8+16.6=49.4,
4.4+6.7=11.1, 23.2-0.9=22.3, 26÷10=2.6,
21.2+1.3=22.5, 9.2+2.9=12.1, 7.6-2.1=5.5.

Bicycling
True, False, False, True, False, True, False.

Body parts
Muscle, skin, heart, lung, eye, toe, blood, bone. SKELETON.

Keep cool
Midnight, 40°C, midday, 37.5°C, 38.5°C, 1 degree.

Computer confusion
hardware, chip, byte, mouse, screen, computer, program, printer, software.

Two by two
Megabyte

Fast cars
200mph=320km/h, 230mph=368km/h, 146mph=233.6km/h,
300mph=480km/h, 430mph=688km/h,
622mph=995.2km/h, 633mph=1012.8km/h.

ANSWERS

Slow sums
1. a) 6 hours b) 3hrs c) 1 hrs
2. a) 3 hours b) 1½hrs c) ½hr
3. a) 1 hour b) ½hr c) 10 minutes

TV Times
1. 1pm, 40mins. 2. 2hrs. 3. 1h 20mins. 4. 2hrs 40mins.
5. Treasure Island. 6. 2hrs.

In the picture
two, invented, pictures, screen, lasted, minute, years, best, their.

Sail away
Silver

Treasure hunt
Gold

Call costs
1. £1.20
2. 15p
3. £1.20
4. £1.75

Telephone tangle
microphone, mobile, conversation, network, electrical, automatic, button, modem.

Odd-one-out
toaster, oven, microphone, iron, telephone, oven, light bulb, bicycle.
4, 7, 13, 8, 16, 9.

CLUES

Rocket riddle
Write down all the possible letters and then begin to work out a word that makes sense. For example the first letter could be m or r, the second p,o or b. The second letter must be 'o' because that is the only one of the three letters p,o,b which can follow m or r. So now you have 'mo' or 'ro'. Keep going!

For the code, use the white paper on the inside cover of this book to write the letters of the code under the word, so that it looks like this

A S T R O N O M E R
B Z L M X T X E R M

Flying high
write the problem out carefully like this: 19 811
                            8 848

To the point
Draw a line under the problem and put the decimal point in exactly the same place in the answer, e.g. 34.3
                 5.8

To divide by 10 just move the decimal point one place to the left, e.g. $26 \div 10 = 26.0 \div 10 = 2.6$

Slow sums
4mph means 4 miles in one hour. To travel 12 miles at 4mph it will take $12 \div 4 = 3$ hours
To travel 12 miles at 24 mph it will take $12 \div 24 = \frac{1}{2}$ hour

Call costs
Be careful to chose the right table for the time of the call. Then decide if it's local, regional or national.

Telephone tangle
If you get stuck, go on to the next.

Odd-one-out
Here is a word to help you with each one.
1. cold
2. clothes
3. recordings
4. food
5. entertainment
6. loudspeakers
7. heating
8. engines